WILD DOGS

PAST & PRESENT

KELLY MILNER HALLS

DARBY CREEK PUBLISHING

To Charles, a Great Dane with regal distinction who taught me how to really love a dog. To Yogi, a domesticated giant with the heart and spirit of these wonderful wild dogs. His memory survives. To Cricket, a faithful, crippled mutt who healed my heart before she said goodbye. And to little Gizmo, a tired, old eight-pounder, not long for this world, who will doubtless run with Charles, Yogi, and Cricket when he gets to the other side. Thanks for bettering my world. ~ KMH

———————————————— ◆ ————————————————

Cataloging-in-Publication

Halls, Kelly Milner, 1957-
Wild dogs : past and present / by Kelly Milner Halls.
    p. ; cm.
ISBN 13: 978-1-58196-027-1
ISBN 10: 1-58196-027-1
Ages 11 & up.—Includes bibliographical references (p.62) and index.—Summary: Not all dogs are the playful pets we pamper; meet the WILD dogs. Wild dogs have fascinated humankind for thousands of years. Each species has its own tale—from being worshipped to being feared as a ravaging monster. What is fiction and what is fact about these furry animals?
1. Wild dogs-Juvenile literature. 2. Canidae-Juvenile literature. [1. Wild dogs. 2. Dog family (Mammals)] I. Title.
QL737.C22 H35 2005
599.77 dc22
OCLC: 57346929

Darby Creek Publishing
7858 Industrial Parkway
Plain City, OH 43064
www.darbycreekpublishing.com

Printed in the United States of America

2 4 6 8 10 9 7 5 3 1

1-58196-027-1

CONTENTS

WILD BEGINNINGS

Take a good look at the family dog. Man's best friend comes in all shapes and sizes. Some have short hair, some have long hair, and some have no hair at all! From gentle lap dogs to ferocious guard dogs, our canine pets have an assortment of personalities, too. But underneath the fur and tail wagging, all dogs have some basic things in common.

According to scientists, every single dog, from the king-sized Great Dane to a teeny teacup poodle, has come from the same descendant: the wolf. Long before humans had puppies as pets, wolves were howling at the moon. And long before that, the wolves' prehistoric relatives roamed the earth. Today's wild dogs—and ultimately our pampered pets, too—came from those animals.

Dogs in Trees?

So, how did this ancient story begin? Begin by picturing prehistoric North America. The thunder of dinosaurs is long gone, and the screams of flying reptiles have vanished from the air. Dense forests and all varieties of animals cover the landscape. Prehistoric dogs take their first steps into natural history. Scientists believe that may have been as long as sixty million years ago!

The first mammals in the dog-descendant line were called creodonts. Experts think these odd animals actually lived in trees. They didn't look like today's dogs. In fact, you'd be surprised if you saw them. Some looked like weasels (*Hyaenodon*). Some looked a little like bears (*Sarkastodon*).

Skull of ancient creodont

How do we know they were the ancestors of dogs? The proof is in their ears and their teeth. Like today's dogs, the inner ears of creodonts had bones filled with air pockets. Air helps amplify sound waves and makes them seem louder. Creodonts probably heard exceptionally well, better than most other animals in their prehistoric world. Today's wild and domestic dogs have keen hearing, too. Even more important, creodonts were the first mammals to have scissor-like teeth (for cutting) and bone-crushing teeth (for grinding). Dogs also have both kinds of teeth.

Cat-Dogs: Not Just a Cartoon

Before there were cats and dogs, miacids, like *Tapocyon*, had characteristics of both cats and dogs. According to paleontologist J. Lynett Gillette, miacids retracted their claws like a cat, and they chewed their prey like a dog—with molar teeth formed for crushing. Eventually the evolutionary tree branched. Cats and dogs have been on separate paths ever since.

ANCIENT DOG DAYS

Fossil records indicate that the last of the creodonts went extinct about seven million years ago. But before they did, three new branches sprouted from one side of their family tree. Those three animal families—hesperocyonines, borophagines, and canines—were the first real prehistoric dogs. Two of those families went the way of the dinosaurs. They slipped into extinction. But the third evolved to become modern wild dogs—and the great-great-great-great-great-great-great-great-grandparents of our favorite pups.

Borophaginae

FOXY LITTLE "HESPEROCYON"

Meet one of the wild dog family's first members: *Hesperocyon*. A little bit "foxy" and a little bit ferret-like, this small mammal was about 21 inches long. That's about the size of a modern house cat (minus the tail). But don't let the size fool you. It was muscular and very quick. Like creodonts, it probably climbed trees. *Hesperocyon*'s long tail would have helped with balance. Its shock-absorbing, padded feet would have taken the impact of jumping to the ground. This little guy even walked on its toes, like modern dogs. No one knows why, but all of the hesperocyonines went extinct about 15 million years ago.

Hesperocyon

Packs of Giant Bear-Dogs

As big as a grizzly bear (that's about 12 feet long and 1,800 pounds), *Epicyon* roamed from Texas to Montana about 30 million years ago. This giant of the borophagine family ate only animals as big as it was. At that time, this would have included plant-eating mammals like *Synthetoceras*, a prehistoric camel. *Epicyon*'s preference for big game was probably its undoing.

According to UCLA scientist Dr. Blaire Van Valkenburgh, hunting big animals worked for these ancient dogs as long as their prey thrived in large herds. Large herds of grazing animals need to eat lots and lots of plants. Over time, the earth's cooling climates caused the area's plants to thin out. The food cycle was in danger. Grass-eating animals began to starve, and fewer of them survived. As their herds got smaller and smaller, the meat-eating borophagines had less to eat, so they began to disappear, too. One group's extinction led to the disappearance of the other.

Two families died out, but one group of mammals was left: the canid family. Its offspring were destined to become the wild and domesticated dogs of today.

The canid called Epicyon, *the size of a large wolf, attacks a horned herbivore.*

7

THE CANINE CONNECTION

Canids survived the prehistoric era and were more dog-like than any group before them. Species within this group, such as the dire wolf, were not as small as the ferret-like *Hesperocyon*. They weren't as ferocious as the giant *Epicyon*. And they weren't particular about their meals. Canids had an appetite for all kinds of vittles. If large animals were around, the canids hunted in packs and took down the big prey. However, if only small meals were within reach, they munched on these snacks. They weren't picky. Rodents, lizards, and insects would do if these ancient dogs were really hungry. Not limiting themselves to meat, canids even filled their bellies with plants when animals were scarce. Scientist Dr. Van Valkenburgh calls that "nutritional diversity." She says this flexibility kept the prehistoric canid families alive, allowing them to survive and evolve.

DIRE WOLVES: FAMILIAR FACES

When we look at drawings of the dire wolf *(Canis dirus)*, we see something familiar. That's because the extinct dire wolf looks very much like the modern gray wolf *(Canis lupus)*, an animal that is endangered and in recovery today. Both the dire and gray wolf measure roughly 5 feet (or 1.5 meters) long. Both tip the scales at about 110 pounds (50 kilograms). They look like the same breed of wild dog. But some subtle differences set them apart.

The dire wolf roamed the earth about 16,000 years ago, before and as the gray wolf was evolving. The dire wolf's skull was broader, but its

© 1987 Mark Hallett

dire wolf
(Canis dirus)

brain was smaller, indicating it might have been less intelligent. Its legs were shorter and sturdier than the gray wolf's, so it probably wasn't as swift. But the real differences were in the dire wolf's teeth. They were considerably larger than the gray wolf's.

Ten thousand years ago, the dire wolf went extinct, but experts aren't sure why. Some believe early man may have killed too many dire wolves for food or for their thick, warm, protective fur. Others believe a climate change drove the dire wolves' prey into extinction, leaving the dire wolves with little to eat. In a short time, the ancient wolf soon disappeared from existence.

Regardless of the cause, the dire wolf is now gone. But it is not forgotten. Its amazing history can be explored in fossil exhibits in museums. Studies are underway to find connections between the dire wolf and its modern offspring, the gray wolf. Many other canine species have evolved over time, as well. Today a variety of wild dogs—35 species in all—share our world. They live on every major land mass on Earth, except Antarctica. From the largest gray wolf to the smallest fennec fox, traces of DNA connect the doggie dots and give us a picture of this wild and wonderful family.

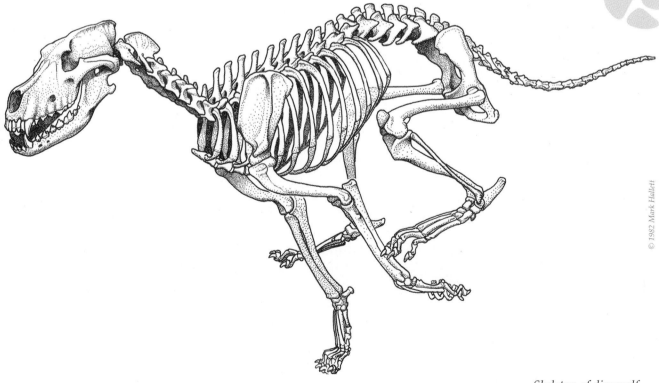

© 1982 Mark Hallett

Skeleton of dire wolf

How Do We Know About These Prehistoric Pooches?

It's all in the dog bones—fossils, that is. Three sites have been especially valuable in teaching scientists about these four-legged creatures: the Ashfall Fossil Beds in Royal, Nebraska; the John Day Fossil Beds in Kimberly, Oregon; and in the oozing tar pits of La Brea, California.

Powdered Glass in Nebraska

Fossilized dire wolf tooth   *Fossilized wolf bones*

According to scientists, about twelve million years ago a powerful volcano in Nebraska belched out a blanket of ash. The experts call the ash "powdered glass." Seventeen different prehistoric species of animals—including three kinds of ancient dogs (*Leptocyon*, *Cynarctus* and *Aelurodon*)—were drinking from a watering hole when the dangerous ash began to fall like toxic snow. The powder was so fine (finer than baby powder) that the animals breathed it into their lungs. As the ash settled in their lungs, the smaller animals started to die first. Larger animals fell about five weeks later. As their lifeless bodies lay in the muddy water, the same ash that killed them also covered them. That led to their bones becoming fossilized. First excavated in 1991, Ashfall Fossil Beds State Historical Park is a popular tourist attraction in Royal, Nebraska, and a great place to learn more about prehistoric dogs.

Ancient wolf skull

Bone Rush in the Wild West

The John Day Fossil Beds National Monument in Kimberly, Oregon, is also a volcanic bone bed. Here a dozen different kinds of prehistoric dogs, including the little *Hesperocyon*, once lived. The fossilized bones and teeth of ancient bear-dogs also have been unearthed there. Discovered in 1864 by Reverend Thomas Condon, the fossil discovery impressed one of the leading "bone hunters" of the day: Othniel C. Marsh of Yale University.

Oozing Treasure in La Brea

In fossil-rich Rancho La Brea in Los Angeles, California, evidence of thousands of the earth's oldest wolves—called dire wolves—was just waiting to be discovered. Rancho La Brea is better known as the La Brea Tar Pits. It is one of the most amazing examples of natural asphalt pools on earth. Thousands of years ago, prehistoric canines slipped into the bubbling pits of ooze. Unable to escape the sticky traps, the wolves were swallowed by the pools and became fossilized by the natural asphalt.

More dire wolves have been excavated or removed from the Los Angeles landmark than any other mammal. Because so many remains were found, scientists believe these ancestors of today's wolves hunted in packs, much as their modern cousins do now. Bones with healed breaks are evidence that the dire wolves sometimes took down animals bigger than they were—animals that fought off predators with thunderous kicks.

The La Brea Tar Pits contain more than three million fossils from the earth's last Ice Age. Fossils are displayed at La Brea's Page Museum, where visitors can watch newfound specimens being cleaned and repaired.

La Brea Tar Pits in ancient times

WILD DOGS OF THE WORLD

When scientists group an organism, they follow a system that describes it in a general-to-specific manner. This system is called taxonomy. All dogs—wolves, foxes, jackals, dingos, wild dogs, and domesticated dogs—are in the Canidae family.

Being in the same family means that in the most basic ways, all dogs are alike. They are mammals, which means they give birth to live young, nurse their young with milk, and are covered with fur or hair. They are carnivores, or meat-eaters. (Some also eat plants when they are hungry, but meat is their primary food.) They are four-footed animals that walk on their toes and do not (usually) have retractable claws. They have well-developed teeth specialized for cutting and tearing. Up to this point, a dog is a dog is a dog.

Beyond the basics, though, dogs begin to differ. That is where the taxonomy gets more specific. The genus and species together form the scientific name for each different kind of animal.

For example, the gray wolf's scientific name is *Canis lupus*, Latin for "wolf dog." The coyote is *Canis latrans*, Latin for "barking dog." The red fox is *Vulpes vulpes*, Latin for "fox fox." That means that the gray wolf and coyote are more genetically alike than either of them is to the red fox. As you read about different wild dogs in this book, you will see the scientific name for each one. The chart on the following page shows many of the Canidae family members you will meet.

Kingdom	Phylum	Class	Order	Family	Genus	Species	Common Name
Animalia	Chordata	Mammalia	Carnivora	Canidae	Canis	lupus	gray wolf
						latrans	coyote
						rufus	red wolf
						simensis	Ethiopian jackal (wolf)
						dingo	dingo
						aureus	golden jackal
						adustus	side-striped jackal
						mesomelas	black-backed jackal
					Lycaon	pictus	African wild dog
					Cuon	alpinus	dhole
					Speothos	venaticus	bush dog
					Chrysocyon	brachyurus	maned wolf
					Vulpes	vulpes	red fox
						aelos	kit fox
						chama	cape fox
					Alopex	lagopus	Arctic fox
					Fennecus	zerda	fennec fox
					Pseudalopex	culpaeus	culpeo fox, or zorro
					Otocyon	megalotis	bat-eared fox
					Urocyon	cinereoargenteus	gray fox
					Nycteruetes	procyonoides	raccoon dog

Gray Wolf

Coyote

Red Wolf

Ethiopian Jackal

Dingo

Golden Jackal

Side-striped Jackal

Black-backed Jackal

African Wild Dog

Dhole

Bush Dog

Maned Wolf

Red Fox

Kit Fox

Cape Fox

Bat-eared Fox

Gray Fox

Arctic Fox

Fennec Fox

Culpeo Fox

Raccoon Dog

Several photos courtesy Canids.org

NORTH AMERICAN WILD DOGS

North America may be the birthplace of the canine species, so it should be no surprise that many wild dogs still live here. From the northern tip of Canada to Mexico, three families of wild canines roam woods, fields, and deserts. These canines are wolves, coyotes, and foxes.

The most common wolf, the gray wolf, is still amazingly similar to its ancestor, the dire wolf. Varieties of the gray wolf can be found in the northern U.S. and Canada. Much less common, the red wolf roams in the southeastern U.S. Coyotes have a larger range, including parts of Canada, the U.S., and Mexico. Foxes, the smallest of the three canine groups, live here, too. The red fox is the most common in North America, but in the southwest desert areas, the kit fox is at home.

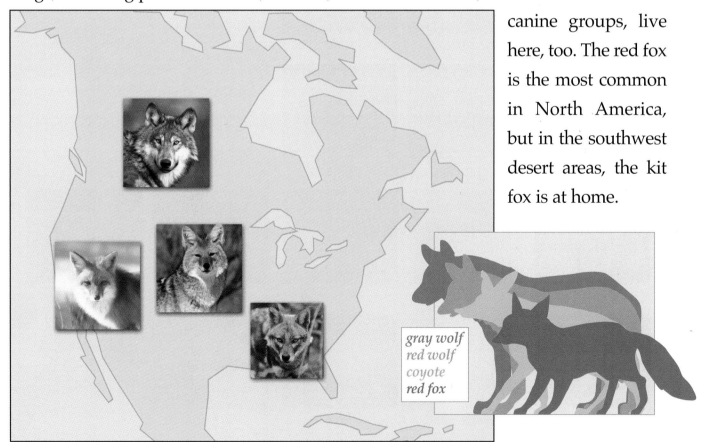

gray wolf
red wolf
coyote
red fox

Humans and wild dogs have had their share of conflicts over the centuries. Today some of these animals are in danger of extinction. Fortunately, like most living creatures, wild dogs have a strong instinct to survive. The more we learn about each species, the more able we are to protect endangered animals. It helps to acknowledge the myths and then replace them with facts.

Name: gray wolf *(Canis lupus)*
Avg. Height: 36"
Avg. Weight: 80-120 lbs.
Geographic Area: Holarctic

Name: red wolf *(Canis rufus)*
Avg. Height: 26" at shoulder
Avg. Weight: 45-80 lbs.
Geographic Area: Southern U.S.

Name: coyote *(Canis latrans)*
Avg. Height: 22" at shoulder
Avg. Weight: 20-45 lbs.
Geographic Area: North America

Name: red fox *(Vulpes vulpes)*
Avg. Height: 20" at shoulder
Avg. Weight: 10-15 lbs.
Geographic Area: Western U.S.

KING OF THE WILD DOGS: THE GRAY WOLF

The gray wolf, *Canis lupus*, is the most common wolf of all. At one time, gray wolves lived from the Arctic to central Mexico, northern Africa, and southern Asia. Today the range—and the population—is much smaller. Gray wolves and some subspecies can be found in Alaska, Canada, limited areas of the United States, and Mexico. Four or five subspecies of the gray wolf exist in North America (See sidebar: "The Eastern Wolf: DNA Discovery"). Very adaptable, wolves are able to live in a variety of habitats, including forests, grasslands, prairies, and deserts.

What does a gray wolf look like? That's not an easy question to answer. The gray wolf isn't always gray. Sometimes it's pure white, especially in the Arctic region. The gray wolf can also be white with gray markings, brown, reddish-brown, and even black.

Of all the wolf species, the gray wolf is the largest. From front paw to shoulder, a male wolf can be up to 90 cm. (36 in.) tall. Its length from tip of the nose to base of the tail can be up to 200 cm. (79 in.). This large, thick-furred animal can weigh as much as 75 kg., or 165 pounds!

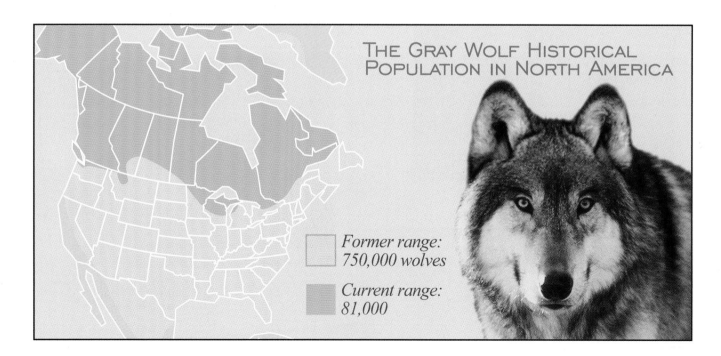

THE GRAY WOLF HISTORICAL POPULATION IN NORTH AMERICA

Former range:
750,000 wolves

Current range:
81,000

GRAY WOLF
(Canis lupus)

Subspecies

Mexican gray wolf
(Canis lupus baileyi)

Great Plains wolf
(Canis lupus nubilus)

Rocky Mountain wolf
(Canis lupus occidentalis)

Eastern timber wolf
(Canis lupus lycaon)

Arctic wolf
(Canis lupus arctos)

THE EASTERN WOLF— DNA DISCOVERY

For a long time, scientists thought only three species of wolves still existed: the gray wolf *(Canis lupus)*, the red wolf *(Canis rufus)*, and the Ethiopian wolf *(Canis simensis)*. Recently Canadian experts have used DNA technology to research the possibility that one of the subspecies, the Eastern timber wolf *(Canis lupus lycaon)*, is actually a new wolf species, *Canis lycaon*. According to Norm Quinn, biologist at Canada's Algonquin Park, almost three thousand timber wolves live in the park. Until this DNA study, scientists thought the wild dogs were a hybrid of the gray wolf and the coyote. After comparing the DNA of these animals with the DNA of the other known wolf groups, experts discovered that these Canadian canines have their own genetic code. The species was given the new name *Canis lycaon*, or eastern wolf.

Similar research is being done on wolves found in India and the Himalayas.

THE TRUTH ABOUT THE "BIG BAD WOLF"

What do you think of when you picture a wolf? If you grew up reading "Little Red Riding Hood" or "The Three Little Pigs," you might think the wolf is a scary animal. Stories have portrayed wolves as bloodthirsty creatures that kill because they're mean. But experts say that isn't true.

Wolves are powerful animals, and they are capable of killing when they must. But they are shy and do not usually attack without a good reason. Unless a wolf is sick or disturbed, it will kill only to defend itself or to get a meal. Wolves prefer to eat wild prey, such as rabbits, not livestock. But a starving pack of wolves will eat a calf or a sheep only if nothing else is available to hunt.

"Little Red Riding Hood" illustration by Margaret Tarrant, 1915.

When a wolf kills for food, nothing goes to waste. It eats every scrap and morsel—fur, flesh, and even bones. Native Americans admired the wild wolf. They believed the animals should be imitated for their intelligence and superior hunting skills.

Werewolves: A "Wild" Imagination

Once upon a time, deep in the woodlands of Europe, sharp-fanged beasts hid in the shadows of darkness. They pierced the silence of night with bone-chilling, mournful howls that seemed more ghostly than real. Their eyes even seemed to glow red or golden. They were the real wolves of Europe's past, and they had local villagers pretty scared.

In the 1500s, people were superstitious and fearful. When unexplained killings occurred in a town, the residents imagined people being transformed into wild animals. Horror stories were told of "werewolves" (German for "man-wolf") that grew fur, fangs, and claws on the night of a full moon and were driven by a mad hunger for human blood. Some individuals claimed to be werewolves and admitted to the atrocities! These days, psychologists have a name for this: lycanthropy, a person's delusion of becoming an animal, especially a wolf. But back then, people called it witchcraft.

When the Europeans came to settle America, they brought their beliefs—and fears—with them. Wild wolves in America's woodlands struck the same terror in people's hearts, but usually without any facts or foundation. In fact, the native people of America admired wolves and had a healthy respect for their hunting and strength. The new settlers did not share those feelings.

Werewolves aren't real, and normal wolves don't have a thirst for human blood. Misunderstandings about the nature of wolves have made people fear them—and hunt them to near extinction.

WHERE HAVE ALL THE GRAY WOLVES GONE?

Fear nearly caused the gray wolf to go the way of its forerunner, the dire wolf. Hated and hunted, this species had nearly become extinct. By the time U.S. wildlife experts realized the gray wolf was in serious trouble, not a single wolf was left in forty-eight of the fifty U. S. states. In 1973 only Minnesota and Michigan (the Isle of Royale) had gray wolves.

Wolf hunt circa 1908

Why had so many wolves disappeared? The main predator was man. Ranchers and farmers in the nineteenth century had been raised to fear the gray wolf. They believed the hungry packs would kill their livestock. They were so sure the wolves were dangerous that they convinced the U. S. Department of Agriculture to pay citizens fifteen dollars for each wolf they killed. Fearing the wolves and needing the money, farmers and hunters grabbed their rifles, traps, and poisons and set out to kill gray wolves.

Before farmers and hunters were allowed to hunt them, gray wolves in the United States numbered about 400,000. Afterward, only about 450 wolves had survived. It was nearly the end of an entire species.

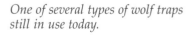

One of several types of wolf traps still in use today.

THE INCREDIBLE, ADAPTABLE WOLF

Realizing the seriousness of this near-extinction, the U.S. Fish & Wildlife Service took steps to save the endangered species. In 1973 the wolves were protected under a new law: the Endangered Species Act. Recovery plans were required in Minnesota, Michigan, and Wisconsin, and they have been successful. For example, fifteen gray wolves were released in Wyoming's Yellowstone National Park in 1995. The following year, seventeen more wolves were released. No one knew if the wolf experiment would work. Would they adapt and thrive—or die off despite the effort? In only three years, nine small gray-wolf packs had given birth to sixty-four new pups! Scientists were thrilled and very hopeful.

gray wolf pups

In March 2004, Wyoming's gray wolves were taken off the endangered species list. Modern-day ranchers started to worry again. "Wolves are killing our livestock," they said, "and something has to be done." As before, some state and federal officials agreed, so hunting the wolves became legal once more. People are allowed to kill wolves that accidentally wander into the wrong places.

In Alaska, where wolf populations are strong, hunting gray wolves has been legal for a long time. The Alaska Department of Fish and Game Harvest Summary reported that between 1996 and 2001, more than 7,000 wolves were legally killed

through individual hunting and trapping. In June 2003, Alaskan state officials made it legal to shoot gray wolves from airplanes. Hundreds more gray wolves will be killed each year because of this new law.

Animal protection groups like the World Wildlife Federation are actively engaged in watching over the gray wolf—and other species hunted by mankind. The future of the gray wolf is in the hands of the next generation.

Good News! Rebirth in Yellowstone

Yellowstone National Park has become the site of a lot of resurrections lately—and many of them are because of the gray wolf. Not a single wolf had lived in the park since 1926, when Yellowstone's last wolf was exterminated. Then, in 1995, fifteen gray wolves were reintroduced there. Since then, some surprises have taken root—literally!

Willows, cottonwoods, and aspens have begun to grow along the riverbanks again. These trees had all but disappeared because the elk had eaten tender young trees before they could grow to maturity. With the wolf back in action, the elk don't hang out like they used to. The elk's numbers are being controlled naturally as the wolves prey on them. As a result of having fewer elk near the rivers, the trees are growing. Consequently, the shade from those trees has lowered the water temperature of the streams. Because the water temperature is lower, more trout are surviving.

National Park Service wildlife biologist and Yellowstone Wolf Project leader Douglas Smith explains, "In 1996, we had no beaver colonies, and now we have seven, because the beavers can eat the low-hanging willow branches." The creation of new marshes by beaver colonies has encouraged the return of otters, minks, muskrats, and ducks.

The return of the gray wolf to Yellowstone has not only saved a species—it has transformed an ecosystem!

aspen trees

trout

otter

RED WOLF RECOVERY

The red wolf, also known as *Canis rufus*, once freely roamed across the southeastern United States. Fossil records show that it may have lived as far north as the Ohio River and into parts of Pennsylvania. Current DNA research shows that the red wolf evolved as a hybrid of the gray wolf (male) and the coyote (female).

Red wolves are not always red, but are often brown with buff coloring and some black. Sometimes red fur grows behind their ears, on their faces, and on the backs of their legs, especially during the winter. The red wolf is smaller than the gray wolf, but larger than the coyote. Sometimes people confuse the red wolf with the coyote, but they have some important differences.

The red wolf is one of the most endangered animals in the world. Only fourteen wolves were pure enough to be used in the captive breeding program. From 1974 to 1980, experts from the U.S. Fish and Wildlife Service rounded them up to protect them and to begin the new program. By August 1997, wild red wolves numbered between 54 and 129, mainly in North Carolina. We know this because when a wolf is captured and/or released into the wild, it is fitted with a radio transmitter. Scientists can use these transmitters to locate each wolf and track information. Another 175 continued to be raised in captivity. Conservationists hope the captive breeding programs will keep red wolves growing strong.

RED WOLF
(*Canis rufus*)

COYOTE
(*Canis latrans*)

RED WOLF		COYOTE
brown with buff, black, red	COLOR	yellow with gray, whitish underbelly
45-80 lbs	WEIGHT	25-40 lbs.
26" at shoulder	HEIGHT	22" at shoulder
large feet	FEET	average feet
massive build	BUILD	scrawny build

Red Wolf Fast-Food Facts

WHO: Adult red wolves.

WHAT: Are omnivorous. They eat meat, but sometimes also consume eggs, bugs, and plants. They prefer moles, mice, rats, raccoons, rabbits, muskrats, nutria, and white-tailed deer. They eat about 2 to 5 pounds of food a day. Scientists know this because they study the animal's scat, or feces.

WHEN: At night. They are usually nocturnal animals.

WHERE: In a home range. Foxes hunt over the same area for 7 to 10 days before moving on to another area within their range.

HOW: Most hunting is done by an individual red wolf or in pairs. Rarely they will hunt in packs if the prey is large, such as a moose or elk.

El Lobo: The Mexican Wolf

The Mexican gray wolf (also called the Mexican wolf or "lobo") is the smallest wolf in North America. It is about the size of a German shepherd dog, weighing between 70 and 90 pounds and standing at about 2 feet tall and 4 feet long. Its coat is a mixture of gray, black, rust, tan, and brown.

Before the twentieth century, Mexican wolves had a large range—from Arizona, New Mexico, and western Texas into Mexico and Central America. Soon more and more settlers moved into the west, and they hunted the same animals that Mexican wolves did. As the wolves' prey became scarce, they had no choice but to start feeding on the livestock kept by the settlers. That led to the beginning of trouble for "el lobo."

Photo: Jim Clark, U.S. Fish and Wildlife Service

The Mexican wolf is listed as an endangered animal. Humans hunted the wolves until the very last wild Mexican wolf in the U.S. was killed in 1970. Now only about 175 captive Mexican wolves survive, living in various zoos in Mexico and the U.S. In 1998 a few pairs of captive-bred Mexican wolves were released on National Forest lands in Arizona and New Mexico. We hope we won't ever again say "adios" to "el lobo," the Mexican wolf.

Howl of the West: Coyotes

Firmly rooted in the U. S. and Canada, the coyote has found a way into the very culture of the people. This scrawny, tawny canine even makes an appearance

in cartoons, artwork, and legends. One poor cartoon coyote has been trying to catch a meal for more than fifty years! He is the modern image of a doomed underdog. In real life, though, coyotes are wild-dog winners.

Coyotes *(Canis latrans)* are smaller than wolves, but larger than foxes. For thousands of years, these shy, 20- to 50-pound animals have been living in forests and grasslands from Alaska to Mexico. Today their range is much larger: throughout much of the United States, Canada, Mexico, and Central America. Coyotes can often be found traveling as packs or as mated pairs, but some also travel alone.

Coyote Conversations

The four most common coyote vocalizations are:

HOWLING: A coyote's howl is high-pitched and often includes several *yip, yip, yips*. The howl is the coyote's most famous vocalization. The message is clear: If you are a male coyote, stay away! If you are a female, come join the clan.

YELPING: If two coyotes get into an argument, you'll hear them yelp. Young pups that are learning to get along in a pack will yelp a lot. Adult coyotes yelp, too, if they get excited or a little afraid.

BARKING: If a coyote senses danger, it will bark to warn other coyotes about intruders. They bark to defend their food, their homes, and their families. In fact, the coyote's scientific name, *Canis latrans*, means "barking dog."

HUFFING: Did you know that coyotes whisper? This is known as huffing. It's a soft warning sound mother coyotes use to call their babies.

We picture this wild dog as a scruffy cowboy's companion, its nose pointed toward the night sky as it howls at the moon. Coyotes are famous for their vocalizations, so this image isn't far from the truth. "Vocalizations" are the very specific kinds of sounds an animal makes on purpose to communicate with other animals. No two coyotes sound exactly alike. According to scientists, coyotes use eleven or more different "phrases" when they talk to each other.

Sharing Spaces: Urban Coyotes

Besides man, the coyote has only one other natural enemy: the gray wolf. Because man has driven the gray wolf out of most of the United States, the coyote is free to roam and increase in number. Coyotes can now be found from coast to coast in the U.S. Unfortunately, that is not good news for everyone.

Coyotes are among the most adaptable mammals on Earth. They have survived because they learn to fit into new environments wherever they go. The same quality gets them in some trouble with man, however. Humans have built bigger neighborhoods and have developed more and more land, squeezing the coyotes' natural habitats into smaller areas. But the coyotes are pushing back.

When living space for coyotes shrinks, the wild dogs' hunting area is reduced. They find fewer animals, such as rabbits, mice, and birds, to hunt and eat. The hungry coyote will leave its territory to find food. Like raccoons, coyotes have come into towns and cities to scavenge

through garbage cans. This wild dog will also prey on small pets just to survive. People consider the coyote a nuisance, but the coyote is just trying to survive.

This major change could have driven the species to extinction. But the coyote adapts—so it survives. Only one in every five coyote pups grows to adulthood. Even so, this wild dog that Native Americans call "the trickster" finds a way to get by.

North America's Foxy Canines

Most of us grew up picturing a fox as a small, red, bushy-tailed, dog-like animal scampering through the open fields. Quick and cunning, it shimmied under bridges and swam across babbling brooks to escape the hounds loosed by hunters on horseback. Tally ho!

That well-recognized wild dog is the red fox. It is the most common member of the *Vulpes* family, known as the "true fox" family. Ten species of true foxes exist worldwide today, but only two of those are native to North America: the red fox and the swift fox.

red fox (Vulpes vulpes)

The red fox, *Vulpes vulpes*, is the largest fox species on Earth. It is native to and common in North America, Asia, and Europe, and was introduced to Australia by British colonists in the nineteenth century. Most red foxes really are red—from a pale yellow-red to a deep reddish brown on their upper bodies and white to grayish on their underbellies. Their legs and ear tips are usually black, and their tails have either white or black tips. Two other red fox varieties exist. The cross fox is reddish brown with a black stripe down its back and across its shoulders, forming a cross. The silver fox can be light silver to black. No matter what color their fur might be, adult red foxes' eyes are yellow.

Red foxes are solitary animals that do not live in large packs or family groups. Although it is much heavier, a red fox can run almost as fast as the swift fox. It can also leap over objects that are 6 feet (about 2 meters) high. The adaptable red fox eats rodents, insects (including worms), and fruit, as well as carrion—almost anything!

The smallest of North American wild dogs is the swift fox, *Vulpes velox*. Sometimes called the kit fox, it can be found in western North America, from western Canada to Texas. This little fox hunts day and night for fish, small mammals, insects, berries, and birds—almost anything it can eat. The swift fox is light gray with orange sides and milky-white belly fur. It is called "swift" because it

Photo: U.S. Fish and Wildlife Service

swift (or kit) fox (Vulpes velox)

can run as fast as 30 miles (50 kilometers) per hour! Until two decades ago, the swift fox was extinct in Canada. Efforts to repopulate the foxes have been fairly successful.

SOME SLY FOX COUSINS

Other canines have the word "fox" as a part of their popular name, but they are not part of the *Vulpes* clan. These foxes are cousins, and they may belong to one of several families, including *Urocyon* and *Alopex*. According to the similarities and differences in their DNA, these animals are classified into one genus or another.

Although not "true" foxes, several other species can be found in North America. The Arctic fox is the only dog to successfully make a home in the frozen regions of the Arctic Circle. They flourish in North America, Iceland, Greenland, and Eurasia, and have also been seen in France, Great Britain, Germany, Poland, and Switzerland. Two coloration patterns are common: white and blue (or gray). In summer, the white Arctic fox turns gray, and the blue fox turns chocolate brown. Only one percent of Arctic foxes are blue. The Arctic fox has small, rounded ears. Its footpads are covered with fur to protect them against frostbite.

Native to all of North America, as well as Mexico and Venezuela, the gray fox is named for the color of its body fur: salt and pepper. It has patches of tan and white on its throat and belly. A gray fox's fur is thinner than the fur of foxes in colder climates, and its legs are shorter. This fox has a special talent: It has retractable claws, like a cat, and can climb trees. Gray foxes are nocturnal hunters and eat a diet

Some photos courtesy U.S. Fish and Wildlife Service

RED FOX	SWIFT FOX	ARCTIC FOX	GRAY FOX	ISLAND FOX
Vulpes vulpes	*Vulpes velox*	*Vulpes lagopus*	*Vulpes cinereoargenteus*	*Vulpes littoralis*
23" - 36" long	15" - 21" long	21" - 22" long	21" - 32" long	19" - 20" long
20 - 30 lbs.	4 - 7 lbs.	7 - 9 lbs.	7 - 15 lbs.	4 - 7 lbs.

Family of foxes

similar to most other foxes, including small mammals, birds, insects, and fruits. They will take fowl (chickens and other farm birds) if other food sources are scarce. Every year, half a million gray foxes are trapped to provide fur for the fashion industry. That is half the entire gray fox population in some states! Even so, their population count remains strong.

island gray fox

The island fox, which is sometimes called the island gray fox, is native to Southern California's six Channel Islands: San Miguel, San Nicholas, Santa Cruz, San Clemente, Santa Catalina, and Santa Rosa. Thousands of years ago, ancestors of these foxes crossed a land bridge with shallow waters from what is now California onto the islands. They evolved independently when the Pacific Ocean closed off their access to the mainland. The island fox is brown to red in coloration. Its diet changes with the seasons, but includes insects, fruits, small mammals, reptiles, birds, and eggs. Federal law protects these rare foxes.

Zuni Animal Fetishes: The Wolf, the Coyote, and the Fox

According to an ancient Zuni legend, the ancestors of man first appeared from the four caves of the underworld. As they wandered out of those dark caves, they faced strange, new enemies they didn't understand. Ferocious wild beasts were after them, and they were afraid. So they called on powerful magic and shrank the wild animals into tiny statues of stone.

Today the Zuni and other Southwest Native American tribes carve similar statues of stone and call them spiritual fetishes. They believe that keeping the beautiful little pieces of art helps the fetish's owner take on the unique strengths and characteristics of that living animal. The Zuni honor six animals as guardians. Each is a symbol of a direction: north–mountain lion, south–badger, east–wolf, west–bear, up–eagle, and down–mole.

The Zuni people believe that wolf, coyote, and fox fetishes have special attributes to "pass on" to their owners. The wolf is regarded as a pathfinder and teacher. To the Zuni people, the coyote is a master trickster who sometimes ends up tricking himself. Owning a coyote fetish,

Hand-carved red fox fetish

then, may help the owner laugh at himself and find humor in his or her own foolishness. The fox is the master of camouflage, cleverness, and loyalty. Stone carvers create fetishes to help remind people to admire and seek these qualities in themselves and others.

WILD DOGS OF EUROPE AND ASIA

Europe and Asia make up the largest landmass in the world. Eurasia (Europe and Asia combined) is covered by millions of acres of woodlands, grasslands, and other wildlife-friendly areas. Some of the wild dogs common in North America, such as wolves and foxes, can also be found in Eurasia. That's because the canines that originated in North America didn't stay there. Land bridges made it possible for the wild dogs to travel into new regions. They migrated from North America to Asia and then continued into other parts of the world. As they moved, they adapted and evolved in order to survive. Some animals in Asia eventually drifted into Europe—and then into other areas, too.

Across Europe and Asia various canines have made their homes. Wolves, foxes, dholes, and even raccoon dogs face the same battles for survival that other wild dogs face. They must hunt carefully—all the while staying alert so they are not captured or killed by human hunters.

Wolves' Secrets to Survival

All wolves, including European wolves, live and hunt in packs. Because of this, they can kill an animal that is more than ten times the size of a single wolf! The wolf is a good swimmer and will chase prey into water if necessary.

Wolves are swift and silent. They run on their toes like a cat, so their heels never touch the ground. This means they can run very fast while making almost no noise. Sneaking up on an elk is a lot easier than having to chase it for miles and miles.

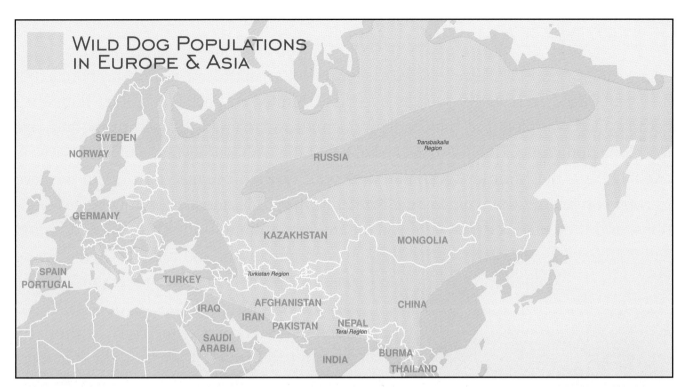

WILD DOG POPULATIONS IN EUROPE & ASIA

SWEDEN
NORWAY
RUSSIA
Transbaikalia Region
GERMANY
KAZAKHSTAN
MONGOLIA
SPAIN
PORTUGAL
TURKEY
Turkistan Region
IRAQ
AFGHANISTAN
CHINA
IRAN
PAKISTAN
NEPAL
Terai Region
SAUDI ARABIA
INDIA
BURMA
THAILAND

EUROPEAN WOLF
(*Canis lupus lupus*)

FOUND IN:

Russia, Norway, Sweden, Spain, Portugal, Germany, Turkey, and Italy

INDIAN WOLF
OR PALE WOLF
(*Canis lupus pallipes*)

FOUND IN:

India, Tibet, Nepal, and Mongolia

HIMALAYAN WOLF
(*Canis lupus chanco*)

FOUND IN:

India, Tibet, Nepal, and Mongolia

RED FOX
(*Vulpes vulpes*)

FOUND IN:

All of Europe and Asia

BENGAL FOX
(*Vulpes bengalensis*)

FOUND IN:

India and Pakistan

© *Mandal Ranjit/NHPA*

CORSAC FOX
(*Vulpes corsac*)

FOUND IN:

Russia, Turkestan, Afghanistan, Mongolia, Transbaikalia, and Northern Manchuria

VERY RARE SPECIES PHOTO NOT AVAILABLE

TIBETAN FOX
(*Vulpes ferrilata*)

FOUND IN:

India, China, and Nepal

DHOLE
(*Cuon alpinus*)

FOUND IN:

South Asia, India, Russia, Thailand, Burma, and China

RACCOON DOG
(*Nyctereutes procyonoides*)

FOUND IN:

Northern Asia, Japan, Northern and Central Europe

European Wolves

Some scientists believe that the first gray wolves appeared in Eurasia about a million years ago. The ancient wolves lived and hunted in packs, and they flourished because food was plentiful. They had few enemies and roamed all over Europe and Asia for a long, long time. Then humans arrived, and the wolf had its first real adversary.

During the Middle Ages, man and wolf clashed because farmers in western Europe considered the wolf to be a threat. In that time, most people were superstitious, and they believed the wolf was the devil in animal form. This fear and hatred turned into myths and folktales, which were passed down from one generation to the next. Over the centuries, people believed they were doing the right thing by destroying wolves. They thought they were ridding their areas of an evil animal. The last wolves were killed in England in 1743 and in Ireland in 1773. Then, following World War II, more wolves were destroyed in central and northern Europe.

European wolf

The surviving species is known as the European wolf *(Canis lupus lupus)*, a subspecies of the gray wolf. This is one of the rarest animals on the planet and now lives in only the most remote regions. The European wolf is almost extinct in western Europe. In fact, so few wolves exist in some areas that the animals have had to adapt to hunting alone, rather than in packs. Wolves have even been seen feeding alongside stray dogs! As a result, European wolves are even more vulnerable to hunters and predators.

Not all news about the European wolf is bad, though. Russia is home to more than 90,000 of these wild wonders. Various subspecies of wolves are now protected in several other European countries, such as Norway, Sweden, Spain, Portugal, Germany, Turkey, and Italy. Wildlife experts are even considering reintroducing European wolves to the Scottish Highlands.

WILD WOLVES OF INDIA, PAKISTAN, MONGOLIA, AND CHINA

Two kinds of gray wolves can be found in Asia: the Indian wolf, or pale wolf *(Canis lupus pallipes)*, and the Himalayan wolf *(Canis lupus chanco)*. The two groups are separated by geography. A wet tropical grassland called the Terai keeps each wolf type on its own side of Asia. Not much is know about either of these wolves. Like so many of their relatives, they also are threatened by hunters and people who fear them. Today about 2,000 Indian wolves and 350 Himalayan wolves exist in India, Tibet, and Nepal.

In some of the largest countries in Asia, wolves live unprotected because they are so far away from human beings. In Mongolia, for example, about 10,000 wolves roam freely. Mongolia is not densely populated, so the wolves live a fairly undisturbed life and are not threatened with extinction. On the other hand, wolves are more threatened in China, where the human population is much larger. They have been hunted, trapped, and poisoned by people. As time passes, the wolves are losing more and more of their habitat. Today they survive in only 20 percent of their original range.

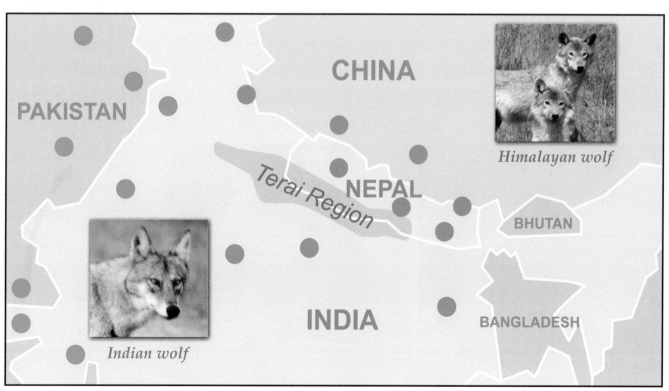

CHINA

PAKISTAN

Terai Region

NEPAL

BHUTAN

Himalayan wolf

INDIA

BANGLADESH

Indian wolf

Eurasian Fox Tales

The most common fox in Europe and Asia is the same little mammal that claims territory in North America: the red fox *(Vulpes vulpes)*. In fact, recent counts show that red foxes may be the most widespread wild dog species in the world. They live across Europe and in Asia from Japan to Indochina. No red foxes live in Iceland, however.

Name: red fox *(Vulpes vulpes)*
Geographic Area: Europe,
Asia, Japan & Indonesia

Other fox families make their homes in parts of Asia. They include the Bengal fox *(Vulpes bengalensis)*, which lives in the semi-desert regions of India and Pakistan. Its color—sandy-orange fur with a black-tipped tail—helps provide camouflage in the desert. Not much is known about this fox because it has been hunted to near-extinction. Scientists believe that pairs mate for life. Bengal foxes eat insects, birds, rodents, crabs, melons, and a few other plants. Adults are 18 to 24 inches long and weigh 5 to 9 pounds.

Another Eurasian fox is the Corsac fox *(Vulpes corsac)*. Its range is extensive and includes the steppes of southeastern Russia, Turkestan, Afghanistan, Mongolia, Transbaikalia, and northern Manchuria. Sometimes it is called the steppe fox. About 20 to 24 inches long and 6 to 11 pounds, this social fox has gray or gray-red fur and a white chin. It

Bengal fox

Corsac fox

hunts in packs and eats mammals, birds, and reptiles. Like the Bengal fox, the Corsac fox is a threatened species.

The Tibetan fox *(Vulpes ferrilata)* is a rather secretive species. Very few people have ever seen one! Its habitats include the high-altitude Tibetan plateau of India, China, and Nepal. Supposedly, no photos of the Tibetan fox have ever been captured, but experts believe they are tan or rust-colored with gray tips on their ears and white tails. The Tibetan fox grows to be 20 to 28 inches long.

FOX FACTS

- A female fox is called a vixen.
- The Scottish term for fox is "tod." (Remember the movie *The Fox and the Hound?* The fox's name was Tod!)
- A group of foxes is called a skulk.
- When a fox is asleep, it gives off no scent.
- If food is scarce, a mother fox will only feed some of her cubs, allowing the others to die.
- Fox hunting is still popular in Europe, but the fox is often not taken.
- The pupil in the eye of a red fox is oval and vertical.
- The Corsac fox was a popular pet in seventeenth-century Russia.
- In Japan foxes are revered. About 20,000 fox statues are found in and near Japanese shrines.

ASIA'S RED DOG: THE DHOLE

In the classic story *The Jungle Book* by Rudyard Kipling, one of the characters is a "red dog" that lives in the wilds of India and Asia. It is the fearsome dhole (*Cuon alpinus*, meaning "mountain dog"). Sometimes called a red dog or Asiatic wild dog, the dhole (pronounced dōl) gets its name from the English/Indian word "tola," meaning wolf. It lives over a wide expanse that includes South Asia, India, Russia, Thailand, Burma, and China. Unfortunately, very few of them remain in some of those countries.

This intelligent, social wild dog looks like its distant relatives, but the dhole is actually very unique. This dog can whistle! After spending the day wandering in small groups, a single dhole makes a warning sound like a whistle when it's time for pack members to join together. The red dog makes other sounds, too, including screams, mews, and one noise that sounds like the cluck of a chicken.

Dholes can take down an animal twenty times their own weight, thanks to organized pack hunting. They eat deer, wild sheep, rodents, and rabbits. Dholes are able swimmers, and they sometimes drive their prey into water to capture them. These little dogs can be fierce and will attack tigers and bears to protect their food and dens.

According to Arun Venkataraman of the Asian Elephant Conservation Centre in India, dholes take good care of each other. In a pack of 5 to 12 dogs, only one female will have pups. The other pack members, very often her older offspring, will help care for, protect, and feed the new litter. In order to raise healthy puppies and establish strong social packs, the dhole depends on its territory. Unfortunately, much of the dholes' range is disappearing as human communities move further and further into the wild.

Like most other wild dogs, the dhole is a threatened or endangered species in some areas. People have destroyed the dholes for hundreds of years because they believe the animals are a threat to their livestock. Local villagers sometimes stole the large prey that dhole packs killed for food. This left the weary wild dogs with nothing but hunger to show for their hard work. Sometimes a population of dholes will unexpectedly "crash," meaning the animals die off with little or no explanation. Disease, poison, or larger predators may be at the heart of these strange disappearances.

Nations all over Asia are working to protect the dhole from harm before it is too late. In 1971 Russia made it illegal to hunt these dogs. The Indian government passed a wildlife act in 1972 that prohibits killing a dhole. In addition, they are protected in Thailand under their 1992 Wildlife Preservation and Protection Act. Several national parks and sanctuaries in Asia protect these animals now, too.

The good news is that the dhole is an adaptable canine, much like its relatives worldwide. In some areas where dholes have not been seen in decades, suddenly a pack will arrive and live there for a while before moving on. No one knows why, but they seem to be saying, "We're here to stay."

It's a dog?... It's a raccoon?... It's a raccoon dog!

Raccoons are one animal—and dogs are another. But what happens when you have a wild dog that looks amazingly like a raccoon? You call it a raccoon dog! Many people in Eurasia just call it a "tanuki." Its scientific name is *Nyctereutes procyonoides*, which means "night-wanderer similar to a raccoon." It should be no surprise, then, to discover that this wild dog is nocturnal.

It begins hunting soon after sunset, takes a break around midnight, and then resumes the hunt until just before dawn. It is omnivorous, meaning it eats both meat and plants. Because of their small teeth, raccoon dogs cannot eat large prey. They depend on mice, rats, frogs, birds, insects, lizards, and seeds for survival. This amazing dog can even safely eat poisonous frogs and toads!

Raccoon dogs put on extra weight just before winter. Then they take a snooze, but not a true hibernation, from November to April. One of their strangest habits is establishing latrines, or "potty spots," which they use regularly. Latrines seem to mark particular territories, too. Perhaps the smell is enough to keep invaders away. That could be important, because the little raccoon dog cannot bark.

Although these "tanukis" have been hunted nearly to extinction in northern Asia, their original home, they are protected as endangered animals in Japan. Some groups of raccoon dogs have moved into northern and central Europe and their populations are spreading quickly.

WILD DOGS OF AFRICA AND THE MIDDLE EAST

Wild dogs have a long—and even sacred—history on the African continent. Prehistoric humans painted images of dogs on cave walls. In ancient Egypt, artists portrayed some of their gods as part-dog, part-man.

But wild dogs didn't vanish with the ancient people of Africa. Today, as prides of lions pad across the savannahs, as zebras drink from muddy watering holes, and as the elephants gently care for their young, canines such as Ethiopian wolves and jackals still claim these rugged places as their home. They will continue to share this land—as long as they are able to survive.

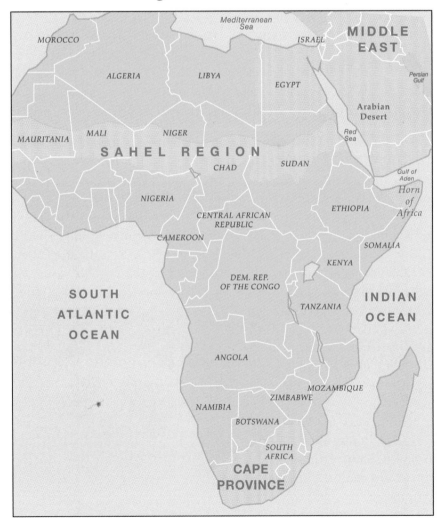

ETHIOPIAN WOLF
(Canis simensis)
FOUND IN:
Horn of Africa

INDIAN WOLF
(Canis lupus pallipes)
FOUND IN:
Israel and the Middle East

AFRICAN WILD DOG
(Lycaon pictus)
FOUND IN:
West & Central Africa

PALE FOX
(Vulpes pallida)
FOUND IN:
Sahel Region of Africa

SIDE-STRIPED JACKAL
(Canis adustus)
FOUND IN:
Nigeria, Sudan, Ethiopia, Kenya,
Uganda, Tanzania, Zambia, and
Mozambique

GOLDEN JACKAL
(Canis aureus)
FOUND IN:
North and East
Africa, and Ethiopia

CAPE FOX
(Vulpes chama)
FOUND IN:
Africa's Cape Province

FENNEC FOX
(Fennecus zerda)
FOUND IN:
Northeastern Africa,
Morocco to Sudan,
and Egypt

BLACK-BACKED JACKAL *(Canis mesomelas)*
Found in Eastern and Southern Africa

BAT-EARED FOX *(Otocyon megalotis)*
Found in Eastern and Southern Africa

AFRICA'S LONE WOLF

Most continents have their wolf species, and Africa is no exception. The Ethiopian wolf *(Canis simesis)* lives on the Horn of Africa, the easternmost part of the continent. Ethiopia's famous Great Rift Valley lies between African mountains and flatlands and the warm beaches beside the ancient Red Sea. (See the map on page 38.) The valley is the home of this endangered wild wolf—and millions of people who are trying hard to survive, too.

A conservation biologist, Dr. Claudio Sillero-Zubiri has made the Ethiopian wolf his life's study. For sixteen years, Dr. Sillero-Zubiri has worked with the Wildlife Conservation Network to protect what is left of the endangered species. According to his research, only 500 of the fiery-orange wild dogs lived in the region in 2003.

Unlike many of the other wild dogs of the world, the Ethiopian wolf's main threat was something other than man. In this case, its enemies were other dogs and disease. In October 2003, people brought their domesticated dogs to the Bale Mountain National Park in southern Ethiopia. More than half of the world's Ethiopian wolves lived in this area. Some of the pet dogs had rabies, a fatal disease that attacks a mammal's nervous system.

Dr. Sillero-Zubiri realized that a rabies outbreak was very likely, so he rushed to vaccinate the wild dogs against the disease. Unfortunately, it was too late. By February 2004, 75 to 81 percent of the park's Ethiopian wolf population had died. Only 15 to 20 wolves survived.

Dr. Claudio Sillero-Zubiri with an Ethiopian wolf

Rabies almost wiped out the Ethiopian wolf. Today all dogs in the area, wild and domesticated, are given the life-saving vaccine. Although the Ethiopian wolf is in serious danger of extinction, the experts who work with these wild dogs remain hopeful that the wolves will endure.

Name: Ethiopian wolf
(Canis simesis)
Geographic Area:
Horn of Africa

© Martin Harvey/NHPA

Pack of Ethiopian wolves

Safe in Israel

In the Middle East, the government of Israel has passed laws to protect the wolves there. Considered to be the same species as the Indian wolf, the Israeli wolf was nearly wiped out in the mid-twentieth century. Farmers and shepherds poisoned the wolves, thinking they were protecting their herds. Raising livestock is very common in the Middle East, so the people have learned to use guardian dogs to protect their animals. These domesticated dogs warn shepherds of danger and scare off the wandering wolves.

Photo courtesy of Bird Holidays Ltd/UK

THE AFRICAN WILD DOG

If you saw an African wild dog from a distance, you might guess it was a hyena. It has the same beautiful, marbled fur—colors of brown, tan, and cream swirled together. Dark brown eyes peek through the mix of colored fur and black skin. These handsome animals live in packs and follow the rules of submission. In other words, they do almost anything to avoid a fight. Each African wild dog pack has one alpha male and one alpha female. The rest of the group respects the pair as their true leaders. When the alphas proudly walk by, the others seem to bow. They lick, they whine, they even crawl under the alpha dogs' bodies to prove they understand who's boss. They work hard to show

© Global Vision International

they mean no harm, because they depend on one another to survive. And these days, survival is not so easy.

Like so many of the world's wild dogs, the African wild dog is an endangered species, but it hasn't been in trouble for long. Only 100 years ago, huge packs of this 40- to 75-pound animal raced across Africa, sometimes 100 members strong. Today, only a few small, scattered packs still survive. Fewer than 5,000 of the very social wild dogs live to fight off extinction.

Why are these beautiful animals so rare? It's partly because they have a "bad dog" image. All animals have to eat to survive, and mothers must feed their young. But nature isn't always gentle in the way it gives life and takes it away. When African wild dogs kill a wildebeest or a gazelle, they tear the animal to bits. It's nature. It's gathering food for survival. However, when people see the African wild dogs kill another animal, they become afraid of the aggressiveness of the canines. They in turn kill the wild dogs without much guilt. African wild dogs also die

because of diseases, such as rabies and canine distemper, carried by domesticated dogs. Some wild dogs also are killed by cars traveling over roads that cut through their territory.

Today, John McNutt, founder of the Botswana Wild Dog Research Project, is trying to help African wild dogs survive. McNutt and others have begun a BioFence program that uses the urine of wild dogs to keep them safe. Like most canines, African wild dogs mark their territory by spraying urine. The urine sends a message to other animals to "stay away." The urine of African wild dogs is placed near areas where humans live. This "BioFence" sends a chemical communication to the wild dogs to keep out—and stay safely away from the humans who would hunt them to extinction.

The Hyena's Last Laugh

What looks like a dog and acts like a dog but is more like a cat? A hyena! The hyena is not a member of the *Canidae* family, so it isn't a dog. Hyenas belong to the *Hyaenidae* family, which branched off the feline family tree long ago. Some experts consider the hyena to be an evolutionary "link" between dogs and cats, but it is more closely related to cats.

Four species of hyenas exist today. They are the spotted, striped, and brown hyenas and the aardwolf. The spotted hyena is the one most people think of as "the laughing hyena." It is a very noisy animal. When it gets excited or scared, it makes a chuckling sound. Some female hyenas have been known to purr while nursing their pups. But hyenas aren't light-hearted. They can viciously attack and kill prey, including large animals like lions and zebras. And they aren't laughing!

brown hyena

aardwolf   spotted hyena   striped hyena

43

THE JACKAL: DOG OF EGYPT

Few wild dogs have as much mystery and mythology associated with them as the jackal. Its night wandering and haunting cries made it the inspiration for Anubis, the Egyptian god of the dead. In paintings and carvings, Anubis is portrayed as a man with the head of a jackal. He was considered the creator of embalming and mummification. The connection between the jackal and death is not surprising. Jackals are scavengers, animals that feed on garbage and dead, decaying flesh. They were often seen near graves, tombs, and carcasses.

But what is the jackal like today, and how has it managed to survive? Three different kinds of jackals live in eastern Africa: the golden, or common jackal; the side-striped jackal; and the black-backed, or silver-backed jackal. None of these sharp-eyed canines are very big. They grow to between 24 and 42 inches long and weigh only 15 to 35 pounds. The golden jackal makes its home in the open grasslands of Africa, whereas the side-striped jackal prefers living near water and hiding in the bushy plants nearby. The black- or silver-backed jackal lives in the woodlands and savannahs.

Carving of Anubis

Although they each prefer a different kind of habitat, it's not easy for any of them to get by. The successful life of a jackal requires cunning and enough energy to feed a constant hunger. They have to keep an eye out for their predators: leopards, hyenas, and eagles, which prey on jackal pups. Sometimes jackals even have to watch out for other jackals. For example, when a mother jackal goes out to get supper for her pups, another jackal might be waiting for the chance to make a meal of her little ones. Jackals don't seem to mind munching on their own species.

Special learned skills and instinctual habits have improved the jackal's chances of surviving. For example, jackals mate for life. This allows one adult to stay with the pups while the other searches for food. Although jackals usually live in pairs, sometimes grown pups stay close to their parents, acting as helpers to hunt for and protect new litters. Nocturnal animals, the jackals usually lay low during the day and

Jackals can be noisy. They yip to each other when it's time to come together.
Sometimes they scream or howl like a siren to tell the pack that they've located food.

wait for the cover of night to venture out for food.

Food can be just about anything that's convenient. Jackals have learned to eat what they can find, rather than holding out for their favorite foods. Being that flexible means they have had to learn a wide range of hunting skills, from grasshopper gobbling to berry chomping to ganging up on a gazelle. And if live food isn't available, then they are just as satisfied to feast on dead animals that others have abandoned. This flexibility has helped jackals survive.

Ancient Gods and Cities

The Egyptians were fond of their dogs—and often worshipped gods that were half-man, half-dog. Ancient cemeteries and tombs have included family dogs, mummified and buried with their owners. Records show that some Egyptians even shaved their heads as a sign of mourning when a family dog died. One of the most honored gods of the Egyptians was Anubis, the god of the dead. Images of Anubis show him as half-man and half-dog or jackal. He was considered the creator of embalming and mummification.

In Egypt, Hardai was the city of Anubis. The Greeks referred to Hardai as Cynopolis, which means "dog city." Some of the largest ancient dog cemeteries in the world have been found there. Another Egyptian city, Wepwawet, was given the Greek name Lycopolis, or "wolf city." Wepwawet was an older Egyptian god, usually linked to royalty and war. He was often portrayed as having the body of a man and the head of a jackal. Wepwawet's head was often colored white or gray, causing some to believe he had the head of a wolf rather than a jackal.

Mummified dog

Dogs often appear in ancient Egyptian art.

45

FASCINATING FOXES OF AFRICA

The Cape fox *(Vulpes chama)* makes its home in Africa's Cape Province. It is a small fox, weighing only 5 pounds, and is about 22 inches long from its nose to the tip of its silver-gray tail. The Cape fox eats some vegetation, but mostly lives on small rodents, rabbits, and insects. These wild dogs have been known to eat domestic livestock, including lambs, but wildlife experts believe the animals are feeding on carrion, or dead carcasses, rather than killing the lambs. This

Cape fox

species is not endangered, but is threatened. It is sometimes called the silver jackal, but don't let that fool you. It is one of the world's true foxes.

pale fox

The pale fox *(Vulpes pallida)* is a petite, little-known fox species that lives in the thorny savannahs of the rugged Sahel region of Africa. This tiny mammal is about 15 to 18 inches long and weighs only 3 to 6 pounds. Pale foxes are the color of light sand, which helps camouflage them in the desert, and they have black tips on their tails and ears. These nocturnal canines feed mostly on berries and fruits, but they will also eat small mammals, reptiles, insects, and some plants. They are highly social and may live in connected underground burrows.

Sometimes called Ruppell's fox, the sand fox *(Vulpes rueppellii)* is about the same size as the pale fox, 16 to 21 inches long and 3 to 6 pounds. True to its name, the sand fox lives in the Arabian Desert, from Morocco to Afghanistan. It is well adapted for life in the arid regions of the Middle East. Its fur-lined footpads protect its skin from the scorching heat of the sand, and its large ears can pick up the tiniest sound from far away. It has very soft, light sand-colored fur with black patches on its

sand fox

46

face and spine and a white tail. The sand fox often lives in family groups rather than in pairs. Dwelling in the desert, this animal is willing to eat almost anything, including a diet loaded with insects.

The smallest canine in the world, the fennec fox *(Vulpes zerda)* is native to northeastern Africa, from Morocco to Sudan and Egypt. This teeny, tiny fox is only 10 to 16 inches long and weighs a mere 2 to 3 pounds. It is also the lightest colored of all foxes, most often a very pale blond. These true

fennec fox

foxes live in small social groups of up to ten individuals and are specially adapted to desert life. They are nocturnal, which helps them survive in the blazing desert heat. Sleeping through the day, they have a reduced need for drinking water. The fennec fox's feet, like the sand fox, are densely furred to protect their footpads and to provide more traction when running in the sand. These foxes sometimes fight over food, such as rodents, reptiles, eggs, fruit, and insects. But they also play together, as wolves and dogs often do. Fennec females can produce two litters a year. Most other fox species give birth to only one litter per year.

bat-eared fox

It may look like it's all ears, but the bat-eared fox *(Otocyon megalotis)* has some other extras, too. Native to two regions in eastern and southern Africa, they occupy the grasslands and desert regions. Their large ears—up to five inches long—help control the fox's body temperature. Its coloration is similar to a raccoon, and its teeth are different from any other fox species. Because their diet mostly consists of insects (40 percent termites and 50 percent beetles), they have as many as eight extra molars, which help the foxes grind up insects' hard exoskeletons. Mice and lizards make up the last ten percent of their diet. Adult bat-eared foxes are 20 to 24 inches long and weigh 5 to 11 pounds.

DOGS DOWN UNDER
WILD IN AUSTRALIA

Australia is a giant island—a continent miles and miles from other continents. It is the flattest continent and—not counting Antarctica—the driest. Because Australia has been isolated from other landmasses, its plants and animals have developed separately from the rest of the world.

The wildlife of Australia includes some of the most amazing and unusual animals in the world. Many of them are marsupials, less-evolved animals that carry their young in pouches. These pocketed animals—which include kangaroos, wombats, and koalas—do not live on any other continent.

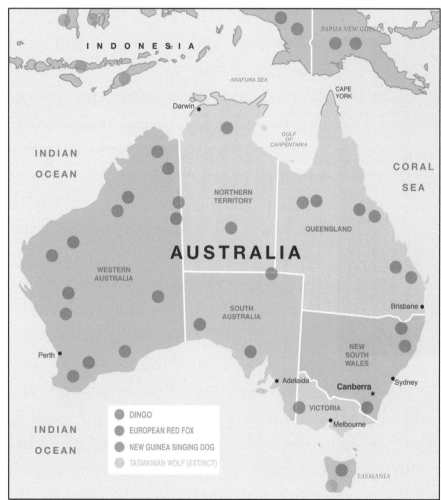

Australia is one of the few areas in the world where no wolves have ever lived. Even the extinct "Tasmanian wolf" was not really a wolf. It, like the kangaroo, was a marsupial. Dingoes and foxes are the only dogs that live in Australia today, and neither of them is native to the continent.

DINGO
(Canis familiaris dingo)
FOUND IN:
Australia, Southeast Asia, Southeast China, Laos,
Malaysia, Thailand, Indonesia, Borneo,
the Philippines, and New Guinea

RED FOX
(Vulpes vulpes)
FOUND IN:
Throughout Australia

**TASMANIAN
TIGER-WOLF**
(Thylacinus cynocephalus)
FOUND IN:
EXTINCT:
Southwestern Tasmania

Monty Sloan / WolfPhotography.com

NEW GUINEA SINGING DOG *(Lycaon pictus)*
Found in mountain forests of New Guinea

AUSTRALIA'S DOG-GONE DINGOES

Canines did not find their own way to Australia. In fact, no dogs existed on the continent before 5,000 years ago. But Australia has a wild dog of its very own—the dingo (*Canis familiaris dingo*). How could that have happened?

Long ago, ancient humans migrated from Asia to what we know today as Australia. With them came wild dogs, which the early humans used either as a food source or as hunting companions. Over time, these wild dogs evolved into the dingoes that roam Australia now. How can we be sure the dingo was part of a prehistoric migration? According to the Australian Dingo Conservation Association, it's all in the bones. The remains of an eighteen-week-old puppy were the first bits of fossil evidence—and they dated back 3,500 years.

Scientists compared the DNA cells in those old bones with 582 pairs of living dogs, including 211 modern dingoes. Researcher Dr. Alan Wilton of the University of New South Wales in Sydney, Australia, studied the results. He believes that a single female from Southeast Asia was the maternal ancestor of every pure-bred dingo now living "down under." Previously, scientists thought that the dingo's great-grandmother was a member of the wolf family, *Canis lupus*. But that puppy's DNA proved them wrong. That ancient Australian pup was more closely related to Asian domesticated dogs, *Canis familiaris*, than to wolves.

Name: dingo (*Canis familiaris dingo*)
Geographic Area: Australia, Southeast Asia, Southeast China, Laos, Malaysia, Thailand, Indonesia, Borneo, New Guinea & the Philippines

Is there other evidence, too? Yes. Dingoes have—and their ancestors had—special behaviors that other wild-dog species don't seem to have. For example, dingoes and Asian dogs never bark, but they do sometimes howl. They also only mate once a year. Most dogs, wild or domestic, have puppies several times a year.

No matter where the dingoes came from, they became an important animal to the Aborigines, Australia's native people. The Aborigines were painting images of dingoes on rocks around the same time the ancient puppy passed away. They valued the dingoes as hunting partners and sometimes as companions. Dingoes were probably the first domesticated dogs on Earth. Even so, today they are wild dogs, and having them as pets is discouraged.

SOME DINGO DETAILS

- Adult dingoes are about 14 inches tall and weigh 45 pounds.

- Aborigines call them "warrigals."

- They live in Australia, but not on the island of Tasmania.

- They live in pairs or small packs.

- Some dingo puppies are born without tails.

- Weaned puppies are fed regurgitated food until they can hunt.

- Wild dingoes do not bark, but they do howl.

A Different Kind of "Wild" Dog: Primitive Dogs

No one doubts that a wolf or a coyote is a wild dog. Fiercely independent, these canines have lived in their own territories without any help from humankind or other animals. But what about the wild dogs that aren't quite so . . . wild? What about the primitive dogs that followed humans and lived nearby, waiting for the scraps and bones to be tossed their way? Those dogs can be found in Australia as dingoes, in Asia as New Guinea singing dogs, and in North America as Carolina dogs.

These primitive canines, sometimes called pariah (pa•rī•uh) dogs, share some common traits. Most of them have shorthaired coats, which are usually ginger or yellow-red in color. Their tails curl over their backs, their ears stand erect, and their muzzles are long like a fox's. Often these dogs cannot bark. Instead they make unusual howling sounds, especially the New Guinea singing dogs.

In the southeastern United States, the Carolina dogs look nearly identical to the Australian dingoes. Recently registered as an official dog breed, the Carolina dog is being researched and protected. Experts want to find out more about the evolutionary genetic code that separated the wolves from the dogs.

Carolina dog, "Hunter"

DINGO IN, TASMANIAN TIGER-WOLF OUT

Four thousand years ago, the dingo wasn't the toughest wild predator in Australia. That title belonged to the Tasmanian tiger-wolf *(Thylacinus cynocephalus)*, which means "pouched dog with a wolf's head." As odd as it sounds, this Tasmanian tiger-wolf wasn't a tiger or a wolf—it was a marsupial. When the dingo came along, the fierce tiger-wolf lost its place in the food chain. It went completely extinct when the last one died in September 1936 in Tasmania's Hobart Zoo.

A photo of a captive thylacine taken by well-known Australian naturalist David Howells Fleay.

Hopeful Australians occasionally report sightings of the tiger-wolf in the outback. More than 300 sightings were documented between 1934 and 1982, including a promising report from near the Arthur River in northwest Australia. Even so, the chance of having this species recover is slight, unless new realms of science step in to better the odds. Using existing DNA to clone the animals is one possibility.

The Australian Museum has had a tiger-wolf pup preserved in alcohol since 1866. Because it was preserved in alcohol instead of formalin, its DNA has survived. Cloning may be possible, at least on paper. Is it likely? Not anytime soon, according to experts. Much more research would be necessary to even try. Decades will pass before the extinct animal has even a remote shot at revival. But as long as that single preserved pup exists, Tasmanian tiger-wolves just might make a comeback.

Male pouch young of a thylacine held in the collection of the Tasmanian Museum & Art Gallery. It was collected sometime before 1910.

Fox Wars

Australia's isolation has allowed many animals to survive without worry, especially the less-evolved species of marsupials. Australia's tiny, pocketed animals—such as the potoroo, bilby, and wombat—lived without being hunted by larger animals. Few predators, and no canines, made their home on this island until recently.

When an animal is introduced to a new region, the balance of nature is usually disturbed. In Australia, the arrival of dingoes long ago caused some animals to become extinct. But in the mid-1800s, the British brought some wild dogs from their home in England when they traveled to Australia, a British colony. These dogs were European red foxes—introduced to Australia simply for sport. Fox hunting was very popular in England, and the British subjects living so far from home wanted to continue this recreation.

Unfortunately, releasing all those foxes caused all sorts of trouble. Foxes love to eat rabbits, so the wild dogs took off for regions where rabbits were plentiful. Unfortunately, a lot of other animals became fox food, too. Native Australian animals that could fly or climb found ways to escape the hungry foxes. But small ground-dwellers were easy prey. Not knowing an endangered species from a common one, the foxes have made the numbers of some rare creatures drop even lower. Declines in the populations of the green turtle, the greater bilby, the bridled nail-tail wallaby, and the night parrot have been noted. Australia's most endangered animal, Gilbert's potoroo, has a remaining population of only 30 to 40 individuals.

Trouble in Tasmania

As a result of the foxes' invasion, some citizens and scientists are protesting the existence of foxes, especially on the island of Tasmania. Until 2001, none lived on Tasmania. In 2002, after several sightings and two possible fox "kills," the Tasmanian government established the Fox Free Tasmania Task Force. Its goals are simple: to kill all foxes that currently live on the island, to prevent future fox invasions, to educate citizens so that foxes will never be permitted on Tasmania, and to study the foxes' impact on Tasmanian wildlife. Foxes may be hunted, poisoned, or altered by chemicals so they will not be able to breed. While this may seem drastic, the control of this non-native animal will help protect other species from becoming extinct.

SOUTH AND CENTRAL AMERICAN WILD DOGS

With the exception of Australia, each continent has its own special wild dogs, and South America is no different. Some of South America's wild dogs look like canines from other regions. One of the most common wild canines in the world is the fox, but in South America this little dog is known as "el zorro." Other members of the South American *canis* family are completely unique. One of them looks more like a teddy bear than a dog, and another looks like a fox on stilts! Alike or different, these South American canines are part of the bigger picture. So let's take a look at these wild dogs that make their homes south of the equator.

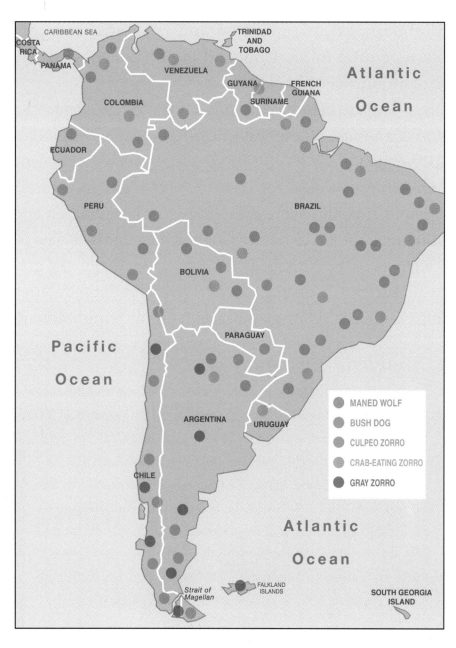

maned wolf

culpeo zorro

crab-eating zorro

"Zorro" is not only a masked hero—in South America "zorro" is a fox!

Left: *bush dog*

Below: *gray zorro*

THE MANED WOLF—A "FOX ON STILTS"

South America's maned wolf *(Chrysocyon brachyurus)* is a bit of a puzzle. It's not a wolf and it's not a fox, but it is a wild dog. Its scientific name means "short-tailed golden dog," but its tail is not short. No one knows how that name was chosen. The maned wolf is sleek and graceful, with long, lean legs and large, prominent ears. It is covered in medium-length, golden-red fur and on its neck is long, dark hair that looks like a mane. The dog's long legs help it to see over the tall vegetation in the grasslands and swamps of Brazil.

The maned wolf doesn't eat like the typical dog, either. Strangely enough, this animal likes to munch on lobeira—a tomato-like fruit—and other vegetation, as well as rabbits and rodents. Sometimes those meals can be hard to find, so the maned wolf becomes a nocturnal hunter and invades farms, searching for chickens and other small animals. Farmers destroy these wild dogs in order to protect their livestock. Maned wolves are easy targets because they sometimes wander alone. These canines mate for life, and when one of a pair dies, the surviving animal stays alone unless he or she finds another solitary maned wolf.

Recently, programs have been started to teach the farmers not to destroy the animals. Some safe havens, such as zoos and regional wildlife preserves, have been established for the maned wolf. In those safe places, the wild dogs can live for more than a dozen years. Even so, these beautiful wild dogs are disappearing. Every year, more and more of the maned wolves vanish from South America because of disease, hunters, and loss of their natural habitat.

Name: maned wolf
(Chrysocyon brachyurus)
Geographic Area: Central and Eastern South America

Canid.org

Magical powers? Villagers native to Brazil once believed the maned wolf had supernatural powers to heal human beings and to bring them good luck. The tooth of a maned wolf worn around the neck was thought to prevent tooth decay—and tea brewed from maned wolf droppings was supposed to cure even the worst cough.

A Dog in the Bushes

With reddish-brown fur, a long torso, and rounded ears, South America's bush dog (*Speothos venaticus*) looks more like a teddy bear or even a weasel than a wild dog. In fact, this two-foot-long mammal looks like it was put together with spare parts. But

the bush dog really is a canine, according to Dr. Pamela Owen, an expert on mammals from the University of Texas in Austin. "The bush dog is the shortest-legged canine ever discovered," Dr. Owen says, "which is a good thing, given its environment."

Short, stocky legs are a plus when it comes to wandering across the soggy wetlands of Central and South America. And when a hungry 12-pound bush dog goes after a rodent in the swamp, it doesn't have to stop at the water's edge. The bush dog has webbed feet! A great swimmer, the bush dog dives right in for its catch-of-the-day.

Everything about the little bush dog—from its skull to its neck to its hips—is broad and sturdy, according to Dr. Owen. But it's the bush dog's teeth that make the animal unique. First, a bush dog has only 38 teeth—fewer than any other known canine. "Those teeth are specially designed for meat slicing, and that comes in handy when it comes to eating large South American rodents," Dr. Owen says.

Which rodents do the strange wild dogs eat? A lone bush dog will hunt two-foot-long pacas (a large cousin to the popular guinea pig), but it takes a pack to go after bigger game, such as agoutis, capybaras, and rheas.

Not much research has been done on the shy, diurnal (active during the day) animal. But we do know they are a very social species. Mother bush dogs give birth to litters of four to six pups. Father bush dogs hunt for food and bring it back to the den, which is usually an underground dug-out space stolen from another hard-working animal, usually an armadillo. That could explain why its scientific name means "true cave-hunter."

The Mark of Zorro

Like other areas, South America is home to many species of foxes. In Spanish, they are known as "zorros." Each species has adapted to its area, causing many variations. The largest fox is about 46 inches long and weighs up to 29 pounds. Some other foxes are as small as 20 inches long and weigh only 6 pounds.

Native to western South America, the culpeo zorro (*Pseudalopex culpaeus*) is the continent's largest fox. Culpeo zorros live in small packs, like most wild dogs, but with a big difference. Males have the top-dog position in most canine packs. But in culpeo packs, the female dogs rule. Every year, maturing females challenge the standing alpha female for dominance. The strongest female takes the territory. Some male culpeo zorros serve the female leader, but most wander off to find mates of their own. When the alpha female finds a mate, she has litters of two to five kits. The father gathers food for the nursing mother and her babies. The average culpeo zorro lives only two to three years in the wild.

Name: culpeo zorro
(*Pseudalopex culpaeus*)
Geographic Area: Ecuador, Peru, Bolivia, Chile & Argentina

This species is not endangered—populations are estimated at more than 200,000. Its presence helps control the rabbit population in the region. However, the culpeo zorro's soft, tawny-brown coat causes this big fox its biggest problem. Every year, thousands of these wild dogs are killed for their fur. Does the fur industry put the wild dog in danger? Not yet, according to South American experts who keep careful track of the culpeo fox population, just to be sure the species is thriving.

Some other common zorros include the crab-eating zorro (*Cerdocyon thous*) of northern and western South America and the gray zorro (*Pseudalopex griseus*) of southern South America. Both species maintain healthy numbers and are quite resilient. The crab-eating zorro is not a picky eater, munching on frogs, lizards, turtle eggs, fruit, carrion, and—yes—crabs. The gray zorro prefers rodents, but will eat up to a third of its diet in berries during the autumn.

FOXES OF SOUTH AMERICA

DARWIN FOX
(Pseudalopex fuvipes)

18" - 22" long
6.5 lbs.

Found in:
A tiny area of Chile

GRAY ZORRO
(Pseudalopex griseus)

28" - 38" long
9.7 lbs.

Found in:
Argentina, Faukland Islands, Chile, Peru

SECHURAN ZORRO
(Pseudalopex sechurae)

21" - 23" long
6 lbs.

Found in:
Ecuador, Peru

HOARY ZORRO
(Pseudalopex vetulus)

24" long
6 - 9 lbs.

Found in:
Brazil

SMALL-EARED ZORRO
(Atelocynus microtis)

29" - 40" long
22 lbs.

Found in:
Northern and Central South America

AZARA'S ZORRO
(Pseudalopex gymnocerus)

25" long
8 - 13 lbs.

Found in:
Brazil, Argentina, Paraguay, Uruguay

The Bald Truth

An unusual hairless dog was worshipped in South and Central America several hundred years ago. During the reign of the Aztecs—from about 300 to 900 AD—a bizarre little dog made its appearance. It popped up in clay figures found in Aztec burial sites and in caves. It was called Xoloitzcuintli (pronounced show-low-eats-QUEEN-tlee) or Xolo, and it was one of the first South American hairless dogs. Aztecs believed this dog was created to be the humans' guide to the afterlife.

Was the Xolo a wild dog? It's hard to tell. Some say it was related to the Egyptian pariah dog or jackal and somehow migrated to South America. It was a pampered pet and bed warmer for some people—and was the meat for stew and holy sacrifice for others. The breed—now called the Mexican hairless—still survives today.

Mexican hairless

FROM WILD WOLF TO PAMPERED PET

We like to think we tamed the wild dog. But some experts believe wild dogs themselves made that choice. These intelligent, adaptive animals discovered that where there were people there was food. It is likely that the canines stayed close to human gatherings in order to collect food scraps and leftovers. The link between people and dogs may simply have been the very thing we still do today—tossing table food to the dogs waiting nearby. The human-canine connection may have begun as long as 100,000 years ago, according to Dr. Robert Wayne of the University of California at Los Angeles.

Over time, people and dogs grew closer. Dogs ventured nearer and nearer, and humans grew more accustomed to having dogs nearby. Ancient humans probably took to raising wolf pups as pets—or as a source of food. Some of the tamer animals began to be trained to do work for their "owners." People kept dogs as guard dogs, as herding dogs, and as hunting helpers. But beyond work, the dogs became faithful companions and man's best friend. A burial site in

bichon frise

border collie

golden retriever

Ashkelon, Israel, holds the remains of a 12,000-year-old man. In his cupped hands is the skeleton of a puppy. Also in that area is one of the oldest pet cemeteries in the world. More than 700 dogs are buried there, each carefully placed in its own grave with its tail tucked around its legs.

Today more than 60,000,000 dogs are household pets in the United States alone—and the number increases every year. One out of every five of those pets was adopted from a shelter.

DOGGIE DNA

How do we know that today's doggie pets are wolves in poodle clothing? It's all in the DNA. In 1997 a group of scientists from all over the world began to look at the genetic connections between domesticated dogs and the gray wolf. UCLA's Dr. Robert Wayne headed the research, which took DNA samples from 140 dogs of 67 different breeds and 162 wolves from North America, Europe, Asia, and Arabia. After comparing specific factors, Dr. Wayne found that the DNA difference between wild wolves and domesticated dogs was less than one per-

cent (1%). Even more amazing is the fact that, when comparing wolves and coyotes, the DNA difference is much higher—about six percent!

Within that different one percent of DNA is the recipe that separates the Great Danes from the Chihuahuas. More than 400 different dog breeds, plus all of those sweet mutts, can look back at the wild wolves in their family line—and howl at the moon with pride.

BIBLIOGRAPHY

INTERVIEWS

September 2004
Dr. Pamela R. Owen, Ph.D., Senior Paleontology Educator, Mammalogist, Fossil Editor, *Mammalian Species,* Texas Memorial Museum, University of Texas at Austin.

August 2004
Dr. Hans Christian Soborg, Director, Alta Museum, Alta, Norway. Dr. Rick Otto, Superintendent, Ashfall Fossil Beds State Historical Park.

July 2004
Dr. Greg McDonald, Paleontology Program Coordinator, Geologic Resource Division, National Park Service, Denver, Colorado.

June 2004
Dr. Xiaoming Wang, Associate Curator of Vertebrate Paleontology, Natural History Museum of Los Angeles County, California.
Dr. Robert Wayne, Department of Ecology and Evolutionary Biology, University of California, Los Angeles.

ARTICLES

The American Zoo and Aquarium Association. "Significant Efforts in Conservation." Dhole captive birth announcement. San Diego, California. July 2003.

"Companion Animals." *2002 U.S. Pet Ownership and Demographic Sourcebook.* Schaumburg, Illinois: American Veterinary Medical Association, 2002.

Courtenay, Orin. "Conservation of the Maned Wolf: Fruitful Relationships in a Changing Environment." *Canid News.* Vol. 2, 1994.

Crellin, David Frederick. "Is There a Dog in the House: The Cultural Significance of Prehistoric Domesticated Dogs in the Mid Fraser River Region of British Columbia." 1995.

"Dogs in Ancient Egypt." *Digital Egypt Universities.* University College, London. 2004.

Environmental News Network Staff. "Coyote control breeds small predators." CNN online. November 17, 2000.

Fox, M. W., ed. *The Wild Canids: Their Systematics, Behavioral Ecology and Evolution.* New York: Van Nostrand Reinhold Co., 1975.

Handwerk, Brian. "Did Carolina Dogs Arrive with Ancient Americans?" *National Geographic News.* March 11, 2003.

Hinrichsen, Don. *Wolves Around the World: The Global Status of the Gray Wolf.* Washington, D.C.: Defenders of Wildlife, 2000.

The Humane Society of the United States. "The Feds Push the Gray Wolf Back into the Dark Ages of Protection." March 26, 2003.

Ives, Sarah. "Is It a Cat? Is It a Dog? Meet the Mysterious Fossa." *National Geographic Kids News.* July 9, 2004.

Lange, Karen E. "Wolf to Woof: The Evolution of Dogs." *National Geographic.* January 2002.

Leonard, Kathyrn. "Going to the Dogs." *Archaeology.* July/August 2001.

Marshall, Leon. "Wild Dog Urine May Be Used As 'Fences' in Africa." *National Geographic News.* March 11, 2004.

Pickrell, John. "Dog DNA Study Yields Clues to Origins of Breeds." *National Geographic News.* May 20, 2004.

———. "Most-Endangered Wolves May Be Saved By Vaccine." *National Geographic News.* September 27, 2002.

Roach, John. "Rare-dog search meets with success, then tragedy." *National Geographic News.* October 18, 2002.

Sacco, Tyson, Blaire Van Valkenburg and Xiaoming Wang. "Pack Hunting in Miocene Borophagine Dogs: Evidence from Craniodental Morphology and Body Size." *Bulletin American Museum Of Natural History.* No. 279. 2003.

Tedford, R.H, Blaire Van Valkenburgh, Xiaoming Wang, and R.K. Wayne. "Phylogeny, Classification, and Evolutionary Ecology of Canidae." *The Canid Action Plan.* IUCN/SSC Canid Specialist Group. Macdonald, D. W., and C. Sillero-Zubiri, editors. 2004.

Trivedi, Bijal P. "On the Trail of Africa's Endangered Wild Dogs." *National Geographic.* December 31, 2003.

von Radwitz, John. "It's a Dog's Life Science." *The Scotsman* news online. October 22, 2003.

———. "New Material of Osbornodon from the Early Hemingfordian of Nebraska and Florida." *Bulletin American Museum of Natural History* 279: 163-176

Wayne, Robert K. "Origins of the domestic dog the fossil record by S.J. Olsen." *American Scientist.* Tucson: The University of Arizona Press, 1985. 74: 316-317.

———. "Molecular evolution of the family dog." *Trends in Genetics.* Vol. 9, No. 6. June 1993.

Weidensaul, Scott. "Tracking America's First Dog. *Smithsonian Magazine.* March 1999.

Wyoming Game and Fish Department. "USFWS Rejects Portion of Wolf Plan." Press Release. January 13, 2004.

BOOKS

Alderton, David. *Foxes, Wolves and Wild Dogs of the World.* New York: Facts on File, 2004.

Greenaway, Theresa. *Wolves, Wild Dogs and Foxes.* Austin, TX : Raintree Steck-Vaughn Publishers, 2001.

Hodge, Deborah. *Wild Dogs, Wolves, Coyotes and Foxes.* Toronto: Kids Can Press, 1997.

Kaplan, Gisela and Lesley J. Rogers *Spirit of the Wild Dog: The World of Wolves, Coyotes, Foxes, Jackals and Dingoes.* Crows Nest, NSW: Allen & Unwin, 2003.

Reid, Mary E. *Wolves and Other Wild Dogs.* Chicago: World Book Inc., 2000.

Sheldon, Jennifer W. *Wild Dogs: The Natural History of Nondomestic Canidae.* Caldwell, NJ: Blackburn Press, 2003.

WEB SOURCES

African Wild Dog. Kids' Planet: Defenders of Wildlife.
http://www.kidsplanet.org/factsheets/african_wild_dog.html

The American Dingo/Carolina Dog.
http://www.carolinadogs.com/index.html

Endangered Animals: African Wild Dog. American Museum of Natural History. http://www.amnh.org/nationalcenter/Endangered/

Australia's Thylacine: Why did the Thylacine become extinct? Australian Museum. http://www.austmus.gov.au/thylacine/05.htm

BBC Science & Nature Wild Facts.
http://www.bbc.co.uk/nature/wildfacts/

The Canid Specialist Group. The World Conservation Union/Species Survival Commission. http://www.canids.org

Dogs: Wolf, Myth, Hero and Friend.
San Diego Natural History Museum Online Exhibition, 2003.
http://www.sdnhm.org/exhibits/dogs/

"Fossil Dogs, Vanished Lives."
San Diego Natural History Museum Paleontology Department.
http://www.sdnhm.org/research/paleontology/fossildogs.html

The Fruit of the Nile: Anubis.
http://www.fruitofthenile.com/anubis.htm

Indian Sun: Native American Animal Symbolism.
http://www.indiansun.net/symbols_animals.htm

Joshua Tree National Park: Desert Kit Fox.
http://www.nps.gov/jotr/nature/animals/mammals/fox/fox.html

Knoxville Zoo: African Wild Dog.
http://www.knoxville-zoo.org/africanwilddog.htm

Kruger National Park, Siyabona, Africa: Wild Dog.
http://www.krugerpark.co.za/africa_wild_dog.html

Laufer, Jack R. "The Wolf and the Native Peoples of the Pacific Northwest." Wolfhaven Institute.
www.wolfhaven.org/newwolfofmyth.html.

Lioncrusher's Domain: Information on Wild Carnivores.
http://www.lioncrusher.com/

Midwestern U.S. 16,000 Years Ago: Wolves, Coyotes, and Dogs.
Illinois State Museum.
http://www.museum.state.il.us/exhibits/larson/canis.html

NATURE: Jackals of the African Crater.
http://www.pbs.org/wnet/nature/jackals/

Ohio History Central: Eastern Timber Wolf.
http://www.ohiohistorycentral.org/ohc/nature/animals/mammals/grwolf.shtml

Old Friends: The Dog/People Connection in the Americas.
PETroglyphs Canine Corner, Summer 2004.
http://www.petroglyphsnm.org/caninecorners/prehistoric.html

Onmark Productions: Fox Spirits of Japan.
http://www.onmarkproductions.com/html/oinari.shtml

Painted Dog Conservation.
http://painteddogconservation.iinet.net.au/Index.html

Recer, Paul. "Dogs much older than once thought, experts say."
The Associated Press. March 30, 2004. http://msnbc.msn.com/id/4264918/

South Dakota Archaeology FAQs. South Dakota School of Mines and Technology. http://www.sdsmt.edu/wwwsarc/arch-faq.html

Tanuki FAQs. Tanuki Enterprises.
http://www.odanuki.com/Gallery/tanuki.htm

Toronto Zoo, Dholes.
http://www.torontozoo.com/meet_animals/details.asp?nav=3&AnimalId=364

University of Michigan Museum of Zoology.
Animal Diversity Web: Family Canidae.
http://animaldiversity.ummz.umich.edu/site/accounts/information/Canidae.html

Valdosta State University. Virtual Museum of Fossils.
Hesperocyon cast of skull and jaw.
http://gatito.valdosta.edu/fossil_pages/fossils_ter/m15.html

Walkers Mammals of the World Online.
Johns Hopkins University Press. Family Canidae.
http://www.press.jhu.edu/books/walkers_mammals_of_the_world/carnivora/carnivora.canidae.html#genera

Wang, Dr. Xiaoming. "Origin and Evolution of Canidae."
Natural History Museum of Los Angeles County.
http://www.nhm.org/exhibitions/dogs/evolution/canid_evolution.htm

Wilton, Dr. Alan. "Genetic Diversity of the Dingo." University of New South Wales. http://www.dingosanctuary.com.au/dna[1].htm

Wolf Facts at Wolf Web. http://www.wolfweb.com/facts.html

Working Dog Productions, Documentary Filmmakers. Search for the First Dog (for National Geographic). http://www.workdogpro.com

Wyoming's Gray Wolf Management Plan: A Recipe for Endangerment?
The Humane Society of the United States.
http://www.hsus.org/ace/15757

Yellowstone Wolf Restoration Website.
http://www.nps.gov/yell/nature/animals/wolf/wolfrest.html

INDEX